Mind Matters

Mind Matters

NAVIGATING MENTAL HEALTH AS A YOUNG ADULT

Anurag Anurag

Anurag Anurag

Contents

chapter		vii
1	Navigating Mental Health as a Young Adult	1
2	Recognizing Depression	6
3	Coping Strategies for Mental Health	11
4	Navigating Relationships and Mental Health	15
5	Overcoming Obstacles and Building Resilience	20
6	Resources for Young Adults with Mental Health Concerns	24
7	Moving Forward and Thriving Setting Goals for Mental Health Improvement	29
8	Conclusion: Your Mental Health Journey	34

Mind Matters: Navigating Mental Health As A Young Adult

Anurag Anurag

1

Navigating Mental Health as a Young Adult

In today's fast-paced and constantly changing world, it is more important than ever to prioritize our mental health. The stigma surrounding mental health issues has decreased significantly in recent years, but there is still much work to be done. Young people, in particular, can benefit greatly from increased awareness and understanding of mental health issues. This subchapter will explore the importance of mental health awareness for young adults, specifically focusing on the impact it can have on individuals struggling with depression.

One of the key reasons why mental health awareness is so important is because it helps to reduce the stigma surrounding mental health issues. When we talk openly and honestly about our mental health struggles, we break down barriers and create a more supportive and understanding community. This can be especially beneficial for young people who may be hesitant to seek help due to fear of judgment or shame. By promoting mental health awareness, we can encourage individuals to seek the support they need without fear of stigma.

Another important aspect of mental health awareness is education. When young people are educated about mental health issues, they are better equipped to recognize the signs and symptoms of conditions like depression.

This knowledge can empower individuals to seek help early on, before their mental health deteriorates further. By raising awareness about mental health, we can also help to reduce the prevalence of mental health issues in our communities.

Furthermore, mental health awareness can help to foster a culture of self-care and self-compassion. When young people understand the importance of taking care of their mental health, they are more likely to prioritize self-care activities such as exercise, meditation, and therapy. By promoting a culture of self-care, we can help young people build resilience and coping skills that can help them navigate life's challenges more effectively.

In conclusion, the importance of mental health awareness cannot be overstated, especially for young adults struggling with depression. By raising awareness, reducing stigma, and promoting education and self-care, we can create a more supportive and understanding community for individuals struggling with mental health issues. It is essential that young people prioritize their mental health and seek help when needed, as this can have a profound impact on their overall well-being and quality of life. Together, we can work towards creating a world where mental health is valued and supported by all.

Mental health is a topic that is becoming increasingly important for young adults to understand and address. In today's fast-paced and often stressful world, it is not uncommon for young people to experience mental health disorders. In this subchapter, we will explore some of the most common mental health disorders that affect young adults and provide information on how to recognize and seek help for these conditions.

Depression is one of the most prevalent mental health disorders among young adults. It is characterized by persistent feelings of sadness, hopelessness, and a loss of interest in activities that were once enjoyed. Depression can significantly impact a person's daily life, making it difficult to function at work or school, maintain relationships, or even take care of oneself. It is important for young people to recognize the signs of depression and seek help from a mental health professional if they are experiencing symptoms.

Anxiety disorders are another common mental health issue that affects many young adults. Anxiety disorders can manifest in various ways, including generalized anxiety disorder, social anxiety disorder, and panic disorder.

Symptoms of anxiety disorders may include excessive worrying, restlessness, irritability, and physical symptoms such as rapid heartbeat or trouble breathing. It is essential for young adults to understand that anxiety disorders are treatable and that there are effective therapies available to help manage symptoms.

Eating disorders, such as anorexia nervosa and bulimia nervosa, are also prevalent among young adults. These disorders are characterized by unhealthy behaviors surrounding food and body image, which can have serious physical and emotional consequences. Young people struggling with eating disorders may exhibit behaviors such as restrictive eating, binge eating, or purging. It is crucial for individuals experiencing symptoms of an eating disorder to seek professional help from a therapist or healthcare provider to address these issues.

Substance abuse is another significant mental health concern for young adults. Many young people turn to drugs or alcohol as a way to cope with stress, anxiety, or other mental health issues. However, substance abuse can quickly spiral out of control and lead to addiction, physical health problems, and social consequences. It is essential for young adults to understand the risks associated with substance abuse and seek help if they are struggling with addiction.

Mental health disorders are common among young adults, and it is essential for individuals to recognize the signs and seek help when needed. By understanding the symptoms of common mental health disorders such as depression, anxiety, eating disorders, and substance abuse, young people can take steps to manage their mental health and improve their overall well-being.

Seeking help from a mental health professional is crucial for addressing these issues and developing healthy coping strategies for managing mental health challenges.

In today's society, there is still a significant stigma surrounding mental illness, particularly among young people. This stigma can make it difficult for individuals to seek the help and support they need to manage their mental health effectively. Many young people feel ashamed or embarrassed to talk about their struggles with depression or other mental health issues, fearing judgment or discrimination from their peers.

The stigma surrounding mental illness can also lead to feelings of isolation and loneliness for young people struggling with depression. They may feel like they are the only ones experiencing these emotions, which can prevent them from reaching out for help. This can exacerbate their symptoms and make it even harder for them to cope with their mental health challenges.

It is important for young people to understand that mental illness is not a sign of weakness or failure. Depression and other mental health conditions are medical conditions that require treatment, just like any other illness. By seeking help and talking openly about their struggles, young people can take an important step towards managing their mental health and feeling better.

One way to combat the stigma surrounding mental illness is to educate others about the realities of living with depression. By sharing personal stories and experiences, young people can help break down stereotypes and misconceptions about mental health. This can create a more supportive and understanding environment for those struggling with mental illness and encourage them to seek the help they need.

Ultimately, it is essential for young people to remember that they are not alone in their struggles with mental health. By reaching out for support, speaking openly about their experiences, and challenging the stigma surrounding mental illness, young people can take control of their mental health and work towards a brighter future. Together, we can create a more compassionate and inclusive society for all individuals, regardless of their mental health challenges.

2

❧

Recognizing Depression

Depression is a serious mental health condition that can affect anyone, regardless of age, gender, or background. It is important for young people to be aware of the symptoms of depression so that they can seek help and support if they are experiencing any of these signs. In this subchapter, we will explore the common symptoms of depression and how they can impact daily life.

One of the most common symptoms of depression is persistent feelings of sadness or emptiness. This can manifest as a general sense of unhappiness that doesn't seem to go away, even when things in your life are going well. You may find yourself crying more often, feeling hopeless about the future, or losing interest in activities that you used to enjoy. These feelings can be overwhelming and make it difficult to function in your daily life.

Another symptom of depression is changes in sleep patterns. You may find yourself sleeping more than usual, having trouble falling asleep or staying asleep, or experiencing restless sleep. These disruptions can leave you feeling tired and lethargic throughout the day, making it harder to focus and complete tasks. Sleep disturbances are a common symptom of depression and can exacerbate feelings of sadness and hopelessness.

Many young people who are experiencing depression also struggle with changes in appetite or weight. You may find yourself eating more or less than usual, or craving certain types of foods. These changes can lead to weight gain or loss, which can further impact your self-esteem and overall well-being. It is important to pay attention to these changes in appetite and seek help if you are struggling to maintain a healthy relationship with food.

In addition to emotional and physical symptoms, depression can also affect your cognitive functioning. You may find it difficult to concentrate, make decisions, or remember things. This can impact your performance at school or work, as well as your ability to engage in social activities. Cognitive symptoms of depression can be frustrating and make it challenging to navigate daily life, leading to feelings of inadequacy and self-doubt.

Lastly, depression can also manifest in physical symptoms such as headaches, stomach aches, and muscle pain. These physical symptoms are often a result of the stress and tension that depression can cause in the body. It is important to pay attention to these physical manifestations of depression and seek help from a healthcare provider if you are experiencing persistent pain or discomfort. By recognizing and addressing these symptoms of depression, young people can take steps to improve their mental health and overall well-being.

Depression is a common mental health issue that affects many young adults around the world. There are several causes of depression in young adults that can contribute to their feelings of sadness, hopelessness, and despair. One of the main causes of depression in young adults is stress. Young adults face a multitude of stressors in their daily lives, including academic pressures, relationship problems, and financial worries. These stressors can quickly become overwhelming and lead to feelings of depression.

Another cause of depression in young adults is a history of trauma or abuse. Many young adults who have experienced trauma or abuse in their past may struggle with feelings of depression as a result. Trauma and abuse can have a lasting impact on a person's mental health, leading to feelings of worthlessness and self-doubt. It is important for young adults who have experienced trauma or abuse to seek help from a mental health professional in order to address their underlying issues and work towards healing.

Genetics can also play a role in the development of depression in young adults. If a young adult has a family history of depression, they may be more likely to experience the condition themselves. Genetics can influence a person's risk for developing depression, as well as their response to treatment. It is important for young adults who have a family history of depression to be aware of their risk factors and to seek help if they begin to experience symptoms of depression.

Substance abuse is another common cause of depression in young adults. Many young adults turn to drugs and alcohol as a way to cope with their feelings of depression, but substance abuse can actually exacerbate their symptoms and make their mental health worse. Substance abuse can also lead to other mental health issues, such as anxiety and psychosis. It is important for young adults who are struggling with substance abuse and depression to seek help from a mental health professional in order to address their issues and work towards recovery.

In conclusion, there are several causes of depression in young adults, including stress, trauma, genetics, and substance abuse. It is important for young adults to be aware of these potential causes and to seek help if they begin to experience symptoms of depression. By addressing the underlying issues that contribute to their mental health struggles, young adults can work towards healing and recovery. Remember, you are not alone in your struggles with depression, and there is help available to support you on your journey towards better mental health.

Seeking help for depression is an important step in taking control of your mental health. It can be daunting to reach out for help, but it is essential in order to start feeling better. Many young people struggle with depression, and it is nothing to be ashamed of. By seeking help, you are showing strength and courage in facing your challenges head-on.

There are many resources available for young people struggling with depression. One option is to speak with a mental health professional, such as a therapist or counselor. They can provide you with valuable support and guidance as you navigate your feelings and work towards healing. Additionally, there are hotlines and online support groups that offer a listening ear and a sense of community for those struggling with depression.

It is important to remember that you are not alone in your struggles. Many young people experience depression at some point in their lives, and there is no shame in seeking help. By reaching out to others, you are taking the first step towards feeling better and finding relief from your symptoms. Remember, it is okay to ask for help when you need it.

In seeking help for depression, it is important to be open and honest about your feelings and experiences. By sharing your thoughts with a mental health professional, you can work together to develop a treatment plan that is tailored to your specific needs. Remember, there is no one-size-fits-all approach to treating depression, so it is important to find what works best for you.

Overall, seeking help for depression is a brave and important step in taking care of your mental health. Remember, you deserve to feel better and there are resources available to support you on your journey towards healing. Reach out to a mental health professional, talk to a trusted friend or family member, or explore online resources for support. You are not alone, and there is hope for a brighter tomorrow.

3

Coping Strategies for Mental Health

In today's fast-paced world, taking care of your mental health is more important than ever. As a young adult, navigating the challenges of life can be overwhelming, but incorporating self-care practices into your routine can make a world of difference. By prioritizing your mental well-being, you can improve your overall quality of life and better cope with the stressors that come your way.

One of the most effective self-care practices for better mental health is exercise. Physical activity has been shown to release endorphins, which are known as "feel-good" hormones that can help alleviate symptoms of depression and anxiety. Whether it's going for a run, practicing yoga, or hitting the gym, finding a form of exercise that you enjoy can have a significant impact on your mental well-being.

Another important self-care practice is mindfulness and meditation. Taking the time to quiet your mind and focus on the present moment can help reduce stress and improve your overall mental clarity. By incorporating mindfulness techniques into your daily routine, you can learn to better manage your emotions and cultivate a sense of inner peace.

Additionally, maintaining a healthy diet and staying hydrated are essential components of self-care for better mental health. Eating a balanced diet rich in fruits, vegetables, and whole grains can provide your body with the nutrients it needs to function at its best. Staying hydrated by drinking plenty of water throughout the day can also help improve your mood and cognitive function.

Lastly, setting boundaries and prioritizing self-care is crucial for maintaining good mental health. Learning to say no to things that drain your energy and setting aside time for activities that bring you joy and relaxation are important aspects of self-care. By taking care of yourself first, you can better show up for others and navigate the ups and downs of life with resilience and grace.

Remember, your mental health matters, so make self-care a priority in your daily routine. Building a support system is essential for maintaining good mental health, especially for young people who may be navigating the challenges of mental health issues like depression. A support system can consist of friends, family, therapists, support groups, or anyone who can provide emotional support and guidance during difficult times. It's important to surround yourself with people who understand and validate your feelings, and who can offer a listening ear when you need to talk.

One of the first steps in building a support system is reaching out to those you trust and letting them know what you're going through. This can be a difficult step, especially if you're struggling with depression, but it's important to remember that you don't have to go through it alone. Talking to someone you trust about your feelings can help alleviate some of the burdens you may be carrying and can provide a sense of relief and validation.

In addition to friends and family, seeking professional help is also crucial in building a support system. Therapists, counselors, and mental health professionals are trained to help individuals navigate their mental health challenges and can provide valuable tools and resources for managing depression. Don't be afraid to reach out for professional help if you feel overwhelmed or unable to cope on your own.

Support groups can also be a valuable resource for young people struggling with depression. Connecting with others who are going through similar experiences can provide a sense of community and understanding that can be incredibly comforting. Support groups can offer a safe space to share your thoughts and feelings, and can provide a sense of belonging and camaraderie during difficult times.

Overall, building a strong support system is essential for young people navigating mental health challenges like depression. Surrounding yourself with understanding and empathetic individuals, seeking professional help when needed, and connecting with support groups can all contribute to a sense of security and stability during difficult times. Remember, you are not alone, and there are people who care about you and want to help you through your struggles.

Therapy and counseling options are vital tools for young people navigating mental health challenges, particularly those dealing with depression. These resources provide a safe space to explore and address the underlying issues contributing to feelings of sadness, hopelessness, or anxiety. It's important to remember that seeking help is a sign of strength, not weakness, and can lead to significant improvements in overall well-being.

One of the most common forms of therapy for depression is cognitive behavioral therapy (CBT). This type of therapy focuses on changing negative thought patterns and behaviors that contribute to feelings of depression. By working with a trained therapist, young people can learn new coping skills and strategies to better manage their emotions and improve their outlook on life.

Another option for those struggling with depression is group therapy. This type of therapy allows individuals to connect with others who are facing similar challenges, providing a sense of community and support. Group therapy can be particularly beneficial for young people who may feel isolated or alone in their struggles, as it offers a space to share experiences and learn from others in a safe and nonjudgmental environment.

In addition to traditional therapy options, online counseling services have become increasingly popular in recent years. These services offer convenient and accessible support for young people who may have difficulty attending in-person sessions due to scheduling conflicts or transportation issues. Online counseling can be a great option for those who prefer the anonymity and convenience of virtual therapy.

Ultimately, the most important thing is to find a therapy or counseling option that feels right for you. Whether it's individual therapy, group therapy, or online counseling, the key is to take that first step towards seeking help. Remember, you are not alone in your struggles, and there are resources available to help you navigate your mental health journey and work towards a brighter, healthier future.

4

Navigating Relationships and
Mental Health

Communicating with loved ones about mental health can be a challenging but crucial aspect of managing your well-being as a young adult. It is common to feel nervous or unsure about discussing your mental health with family and friends, but opening up about your struggles can lead to much-needed support and understanding. Remember that mental health is just as important as physical health, and there should be no shame in seeking help or talking about your feelings.

When approaching the topic of mental health with loved ones, it is important to choose a time and place where you feel comfortable and safe. It might be helpful to plan out what you want to say beforehand or even write down your thoughts to help organize them. Be honest and open about how you are feeling, and try to explain your experiences in a way that your loved ones can understand. Remember that they may not fully grasp what you are going through, so patience and empathy are key.

It is also important to set boundaries when discussing your mental health with loved ones. You do not have to share every detail of your struggles if you are not comfortable doing so. It is okay to only disclose what you feel is necessary for your loved ones to understand and support you. Be clear about what you need from them, whether it be a listening ear, emotional support, or help finding professional resources.

In some cases, loved ones may not react the way you had hoped when you open up about your mental health. They may be in denial, dismissive, or even judgmental. It is important to remember that their reactions are not a reflection of your worth or the validity of your experiences. If you encounter negative responses, consider seeking support from a therapist, counselor, or support group who can help you navigate these challenging situations.

Overall, communicating with loved ones about mental health is an essential step in your journey towards healing and self-care. Remember that you are not alone in your struggles, and there are people who care about you and want to help. By being open and honest about your mental health, you are taking a courageous step towards prioritizing your well-being and seeking the support you need to thrive as a young adult.

Setting boundaries in relationships is crucial for maintaining our mental health and well-being, especially as young adults navigating the complexities of life. Boundaries are the guidelines we set for ourselves in how we allow others to treat us, how much we give of ourselves, and what we are willing to tolerate in our relationships. Without clear boundaries, we may find ourselves feeling overwhelmed, taken advantage of, or emotionally drained, leading to feelings of depression and anxiety.

It is important to recognize that setting boundaries is not selfish or mean, but rather a necessary act of self-care. By establishing healthy boundaries, we are demonstrating self-respect and asserting our needs and values in our relationships. This can help prevent feelings of resentment, frustration, and burnout that can contribute to mental health issues like depression. It is essential to communicate our boundaries clearly and assertively to others, even if it may feel uncomfortable at first.

In romantic relationships, setting boundaries can help establish mutual respect and understanding between partners. This includes setting limits on how much time we spend together, what activities we engage in, and how we communicate with each other. It is okay to say no to things that make us uncomfortable or go against our values, even if it may disappoint our partner.

By being honest and upfront about our boundaries, we can build a stronger and healthier relationship based on trust and respect. In friendships, setting boundaries can help us maintain a healthy balance between giving and receiving support. It is important to recognize when a friendship becomes draining or toxic, and to set boundaries to protect our emotional well-being. This may involve limiting the time spent with certain friends, being clear about our needs and expectations, and being willing to walk away from friendships that no longer serve us. By surrounding ourselves with friends who respect our boundaries, we can create a supportive network that enhances our mental health and overall happiness.

Overall, setting boundaries in relationships is an essential aspect of maintaining good mental health as a young adult. By valuing and prioritizing our own needs, we can establish healthy and fulfilling relationships that contribute to our overall well-being. Remember that it is okay to say no, to prioritize self-care, and to communicate openly and honestly with others about our boundaries. By doing so, we can cultivate relationships that are respectful, supportive, and empowering, leading to a happier and healthier life.

Dating can be an exciting and fulfilling part of life, but it can also have a significant impact on our mental health. It's important for young people to be aware of how dating can affect their mental well-being and to take steps to prioritize their mental health while navigating romantic relationships. In this subchapter, we will explore the connection between dating and mental health, and discuss strategies for maintaining good mental health while dating.

One common issue that young people may face in the dating world is the pressure to conform to societal expectations and norms. This pressure can lead to feelings of anxiety, low self-esteem, and even depression. It's important to remember that it's okay to be yourself and to set boundaries in your relationships. Don't feel like you have to change who you are to please someone else. Your mental health should always come first.

Another aspect of dating that can impact mental health is the experience of rejection. Rejection is a natural part of dating, but it can be difficult to cope with. It's important to remember that rejection is not a reflection of your worth as a person. It's okay to feel sad or disappointed after being rejected, but try not to let it consume you. Reach out to friends or a mental health professional for support if you're struggling to cope with rejection.

Communication is key in any relationship, and this is especially true when it comes to maintaining good mental health while dating. Be open and honest with your partner about your feelings, boundaries, and needs. If you're feeling overwhelmed or anxious, don't be afraid to communicate this to your partner. A healthy relationship should be based on mutual respect and understanding, and good communication is essential for building a strong foundation.

Lastly, remember that it's okay to take a break from dating if you're feeling overwhelmed or if your mental health is suffering. Your well-being should always be your top priority, and it's important to listen to your body and mind.

Take time to focus on self-care and to get the support you need.

Dating can be a fun and rewarding experience, but it's important to prioritize your mental health above all else.

Dating can be a fun and rewarding experience, but it's important to prioritize your mental health above all else.

5

∽

Overcoming Obstacles and Building Resilience

Dealing with setbacks in mental health recovery is a common experience for many young people who are navigating the challenges of mental health issues.

It's important to remember that setbacks are a normal part of the recovery process and should not be seen as a sign of failure. In fact, setbacks can often be valuable learning opportunities that help us grow stronger and more resilient in the long run.

When facing a setback in your mental health recovery, it's crucial to practice self-compassion and avoid being too hard on yourself. Remember that setbacks happen to everyone and are not a reflection of your worth or ability to recover.

Be gentle with yourself and give yourself the space and time you need to heal and regroup. It's also helpful to reach out for support when you're dealing with a setback.

Whether it's talking to a trusted friend, family member, therapist, or support group, having a strong support system in place can make a world of difference.

It's okay to ask for help and lean on others during challenging times – you don't have to go through this alone. In addition to seeking support from others, it's important to prioritize self-care and engage in activities that bring you joy and relaxation. Whether it's going for a walk, practicing mindfulness, or engaging in a creative hobby, taking care of your mental health is essential during times of setback. Remember to prioritize your well-being and make self-care a priority.

Finally, remember that setbacks are not permanent and that you have the strength and resilience to overcome them. By staying committed to your recovery journey, practicing self-compassion, seeking support, and prioritizing self-care, you can navigate setbacks in your mental health recovery with grace and determination. Remember that you are not alone in this journey and that brighter days are ahead.

Finding purpose and meaning in life is a crucial aspect of maintaining good mental health, especially for young people who may be struggling with issues like depression. It is important to remember that everyone's journey to finding purpose is unique and there is no one-size-fits-all approach. However, there are some key steps that can help guide you on your path to discovering what truly matters to you.

One of the first steps in finding purpose and meaning in life is to take the time to reflect on your values and beliefs. What is important to you? What are your passions and interests? By identifying these core values, you can begin to align your actions and decisions with what truly matters to you. This can help you feel more fulfilled and satisfied with your life, even in the midst of challenges such as depression.

Another important aspect of finding purpose and meaning in life is setting goals and working towards them. Whether it's pursuing a career that aligns with your values, volunteering for a cause you are passionate about, or simply taking up a new hobby, setting goals can give you a sense of direction and accomplishment. This can be especially helpful for young people who may be feeling lost or unsure of their path in life.

It is also important to surround yourself with supportive and understanding people who can help you on your journey to finding purpose and meaning.

Whether it's friends, family, or a therapist, having a support system can make a world of difference when it comes to navigating mental health challenges like depression. These individuals can provide encouragement, guidance, and a listening ear when you need it most.

Ultimately, finding purpose and meaning in life is an ongoing process that may require some trial and error. It's okay to not have all the answers right away and to take time to explore different paths and opportunities. Remember that your mental health is just as important as your physical health, and taking steps to prioritize your well-being can lead to a more fulfilling and meaningful life. By focusing on what truly matters to you, setting goals, and surrounding yourself with supportive people, you can begin to navigate the challenges of mental health and find purpose and meaning in your life as a young adult.

Practicing mindfulness and gratitude are two powerful tools that can help young people navigate their mental health, particularly when dealing with depression. Mindfulness involves being fully present in the moment, paying attention to your thoughts, feelings, and surroundings without judgment. This practice can help individuals become more aware of their emotions and better manage stress and anxiety.

One way to practice mindfulness is through meditation. Taking just a few minutes each day to sit quietly and focus on your breath can help calm the mind and reduce racing thoughts. By bringing awareness to the present moment, individuals can learn to let go of negative thought patterns and cultivate a sense of peace and clarity.

Gratitude is another important aspect of mental health that can have a profound impact on overall well-being. Taking time each day to reflect on the things you are grateful for can shift your focus from what's going wrong to what's going right in your life. This practice can help combat feelings of hopelessness and despair that often accompany depression.

When struggling with mental health challenges, it can be easy to get caught up in negative thinking patterns. By incorporating mindfulness and gratitude into your daily routine, you can begin to rewire your brain to focus on the positive aspects of life. This shift in mindset can lead to improved mood, increased resilience, and a greater sense of overall well-being.

Incorporating mindfulness and gratitude practices into your life may not be a quick fix for depression, but over time, these tools can help you build a strong foundation for mental health and well-being. By taking small steps each day to cultivate awareness and gratitude, you can begin to shift your perspective and find greater peace and contentment in your life. Remember, you are not alone in your struggles, and there are resources and support available to help you on your journey to mental health.

6

∾

Resources for Young Adults with Mental Health Concerns

Hotlines and crisis intervention services can be invaluable resources for young people struggling with mental health issues, particularly depression. These services provide immediate support and guidance to individuals in crisis, offering a lifeline to those who may feel overwhelmed and alone. Whether you are experiencing suicidal thoughts, feeling hopeless, or simply need someone to talk to, hotlines and crisis intervention services are available 24/7 to provide confidential and nonjudgmental support.

One of the most well-known crisis intervention services is the National Suicide Prevention Lifeline, which can be reached by calling 1-800-273-TALK (8255).

This hotline connects individuals with trained counselors who can provide emotional support, crisis intervention, and referrals to local mental health resources. The lifeline is free, confidential, and available to anyone in need, regardless of their age, background, or circumstances.

In addition to the National Suicide Prevention Lifeline, there are a number of other hotlines and crisis intervention services that cater specifically to young people. For example, the Crisis Text Line allows individuals to connect with trained crisis counselors via text message by texting "HELLO" to 741741. This service is particularly beneficial for young adults who may feel more comfortable communicating through text rather than over the phone.

It is important for young people to be aware of the resources available to them in times of crisis. By familiarizing yourself with hotlines and crisis intervention services, you can ensure that you have access to the support you need when you need it most. Remember, it is okay to ask for help and reaching out to a hotline or crisis intervention service can be the first step towards getting the support you deserve.

If you are struggling with depression or any other mental health issue, don't hesitate to reach out for help. Hotlines and crisis intervention services are there to support you, no matter what you are going through. You are not alone, and there are people who care about you and want to help you navigate your mental health journey. Remember, it's okay to not be okay, but it's important to take steps to prioritize your well-being and seek the help you need.

In today's digital age, online support communities have become a valuable resource for young people navigating mental health challenges, particularly depression. These virtual spaces provide a sense of community and connection for individuals who may feel isolated or misunderstood in their daily lives.

Whether you are looking for advice, encouragement, or simply a listening ear, online support communities offer a safe and supportive environment to share your experiences and connect with others who are going through similar struggles.

One of the key benefits of online support communities is the anonymity they provide. Many young people may feel hesitant to seek help for their mental health issues due to stigma or fear of judgment. By participating in online forums or chat groups, individuals can share their thoughts and feelings without revealing their identities, allowing them to express themselves more freely and openly. This anonymity can be empowering for those who may not feel comfortable discussing their mental health struggles in person.

In addition to anonymity, online support communities offer a wealth of information and resources for young people dealing with depression. From coping strategies and self-care tips to information on therapy and medication options, these virtual spaces provide a wealth of knowledge and support for individuals seeking to improve their mental well-being. By connecting with others who have experienced similar challenges, young people can gain valuable insights and perspectives on how to manage their depression and take steps towards recovery.

Furthermore, online support communities can help combat feelings of isolation and loneliness that often accompany depression. Through these virtual spaces, individuals can build friendships and connections with others who understand and empathize with their struggles. By sharing their stories and experiences, young people can feel less alone in their journey towards mental health recovery and find comfort in knowing that there are others who are going through similar challenges.

Overall, online support communities are a valuable resource for young people struggling with depression. By offering anonymity, information, and a sense of community, these virtual spaces provide a safe and supportive environment for individuals to connect, share, and learn from one another. Whether you are looking for advice, encouragement, or simply a listening ear, online support communities can be a lifeline for those seeking to improve their mental well-being and navigate the challenges of depression.

In today's fast-paced and technology-driven world, there are numerous resources available to help us take care of our mental health. One of the most convenient and accessible options is mental health apps and tools. These apps can provide support, guidance, and even therapy at the touch of a button. For young people struggling with mental health issues, these apps can be a lifesaver.

One popular mental health app is Calm, which offers guided meditations, sleep stories, and relaxation techniques to help users manage stress and anxiety.

Another app, Headspace, focuses on mindfulness and meditation to improve mental well-being. These apps can be especially helpful for young people dealing with depression, as they offer practical tools to cope with negative emotions and promote a sense of calm.

In addition to meditation and relaxation apps, there are also tools available for tracking moods and managing symptoms of depression. Apps like Moodpath and Daylio allow users to log their feelings, thoughts, and behaviors to better understand their mental health patterns. These tools can be invaluable for young people seeking to monitor their mental well-being and identify triggers for depressive episodes.

For those in need of more personalized support, there are also therapy apps like Talkspace and BetterHelp that connect users with licensed mental health professionals for virtual counseling sessions. These platforms can be a convenient and affordable alternative to traditional therapy, particularly for young people who may face barriers to accessing mental health care.

Overall, mental health apps and tools can be powerful resources for young people navigating depression and other mental health challenges. By utilizing these tools, young adults can take control of their mental well-being and find the support they need to thrive. It's important for young people to explore these options and find the tools that work best for them in managing their mental health.

7

Moving Forward and Thriving Setting Goals for Mental Health Improvement

Setting goals for mental health improvement is a crucial step in managing and overcoming challenges such as depression. As young people navigating the complexities of mental health, it is important to identify specific goals that can help us enhance our well-being and overall quality of life. By setting realistic and achievable goals, we can take proactive steps towards improving our mental health and building resilience to cope with life's ups and downs.

One key aspect of setting goals for mental health improvement is to prioritize self-care activities that promote emotional well-being. This can include establishing a daily routine that incorporates activities like exercise, mindfulness, and healthy eating habits. By committing to self-care practices, we can boost our mood, reduce stress, and increase our overall sense of well-being. Setting goals related to self-care can help us prioritize our mental health and make it a non-negotiable part of our daily lives.

Another important aspect of setting goals for mental health improvement is to focus on building a support network of friends, family, or mental health professionals. By setting goals related to reaching out for support when needed, we can ensure that we have a strong system of support in place during challenging times. This can include setting goals to attend therapy sessions regularly, reaching out to friends for emotional support, or joining a support group for individuals struggling with similar mental health issues. Building a support network can help us feel less isolated and more connected to others, which can have a positive impact on our mental health.

In addition to self-care and building a support network, setting goals for mental health improvement can also involve challenging negative thought patterns and beliefs that contribute to feelings of depression. By setting goals related to practicing self-compassion, challenging negative self-talk, and reframing negative thoughts, we can cultivate a more positive and resilient mindset.

Setting goals to work on changing our thought patterns can help us build emotional resilience and develop healthier coping strategies for managing depression.

Overall, setting goals for mental health improvement is a valuable tool for young people struggling with depression. By prioritizing self-care, building a support network, and challenging negative thought patterns, we can take active steps towards improving our mental health and well-being. By setting realistic and achievable goals, we can empower ourselves to take control of our mental health and work towards a brighter and more fulfilling future.

Embracing self-acceptance and self-love is a crucial aspect of maintaining good mental health, especially for young people who may be struggling with issues like depression. It is important to remember that no one is perfect, and it is okay to have flaws and imperfections. By accepting ourselves for who we are, we can start to build a healthy relationship with ourselves and learn to love and appreciate the unique qualities that make us who we are.

Self-acceptance is about recognizing and embracing all aspects of ourselves, both the good and the bad. It means acknowledging our strengths and weaknesses without judgment or criticism. This can be challenging, especially for young people who may be bombarded with messages from society telling them they need to look or act a certain way to be accepted. However, by practicing self-acceptance, we can learn to be kinder to ourselves and cultivate a sense of inner peace and contentment.

Self-love goes hand in hand with self-acceptance, as it involves treating ourselves with kindness, compassion, and respect. It means prioritizing our own well-being and taking care of ourselves physically, mentally, and emotionally.

This can include practicing self-care activities like exercise, meditation, journaling, or spending time with loved ones. By showing ourselves love and compassion, we can build a strong foundation for good mental health and overall well-being.

For young people struggling with depression, self-acceptance and self-love can be particularly challenging. Depression often distorts our perception of ourselves, making it difficult to see our own worth and value. However, by practicing self-acceptance and self-love, we can start to challenge these negative beliefs and create a more positive self-image. This can be a powerful tool in the fight against depression, helping us to build resilience and develop a more positive outlook on life.

In conclusion, embracing self-acceptance and self-love is essential for maintaining good mental health, especially for young people dealing with issues like depression. By learning to accept and love ourselves for who we are, flaws and all, we can cultivate a sense of inner peace and build a strong foundation for good mental health. Remember, you are worthy of love and acceptance just as you are, and by practicing self-acceptance and self-love, you can start to see yourself in a more positive light.

As young adults, it is more important than ever to advocate for mental health awareness in our communities. Mental health issues, such as depression, can affect anyone at any age, and it is crucial that we work together to break the stigma surrounding these conditions. By advocating for mental health awareness, we can help create a more supportive and understanding environment for those struggling with their mental health.

One way to advocate for mental health awareness in your community is to start conversations about it. Talk openly about your own experiences with mental health, whether it be depression or anxiety, and encourage others to share their stories as well. By being open and honest about mental health, we can help normalize the conversation and show others that it is okay to seek help when needed.

Another way to advocate for mental health awareness is to get involved in local mental health organizations or events. Volunteer your time at a mental health awareness walk or fundraiser, or join a support group for those struggling with mental health issues. By actively participating in these events, you can help raise awareness and show your support for those in your community who may be struggling with their mental health.

Additionally, you can use social media as a platform to advocate for mental health awareness. Share articles, resources, and personal stories about mental health on your social media accounts to help educate your friends and followers. By using your voice and platform to spread awareness, you can reach a larger audience and make a positive impact in your community.

In conclusion, advocating for mental health awareness in your community is essential in creating a supportive and understanding environment for those struggling with their mental health. By starting conversations, getting involved in local events, and using social media as a platform, you can help break the stigma surrounding mental health and show others that it is okay to seek help.

Together, we can work towards creating a more mentally healthy community for all.

8

Conclusion: Your Mental Health Journey

As young people navigating the complexities of mental health, it is important to take the time to reflect on your progress. Depression can often make it difficult to see the strides you have made, but by actively reflecting on your journey, you can gain a better understanding of your growth and resilience.

One way to reflect on your progress is to keep a journal. Writing down your thoughts and feelings can help you track your moods and identify any patterns or triggers that may be affecting your mental health. By looking back at your entries, you may be able to see how far you have come and recognize the progress you have made in managing your depression.

Another way to reflect on your progress is to set goals for yourself. By establishing realistic and achievable goals, you can track your progress and celebrate your accomplishments along the way. Whether it's getting out of bed in the morning, reaching out to a friend for support, or trying a new coping strategy, each small step forward is a victory in your journey towards better mental health.

It is also important to seek feedback from trusted friends, family members, or mental health professionals. These individuals can provide an outside perspective on your progress and offer valuable insights and support. By opening up to others about your struggles and successes, you can build a strong support network that can help you navigate the challenges of living with depression.

In the end, reflecting on your progress is an essential part of your mental health journey. By taking the time to acknowledge your growth, celebrate your victories, and learn from your setbacks, you can develop a deeper understanding of yourself and build the resilience needed to continue moving forward. Remember, healing is not a linear process, and it's okay to have bad days. What matters most is that you keep pushing forward and never give up on yourself.

As a young adult navigating the complexities of life, it is crucial to prioritize your mental health above all else. In a world where stress, anxiety, and depression are all too common, taking care of your mental well-being should be a top priority. It is important to remember that seeking help and support is not a sign of weakness, but rather a sign of strength and self-awareness.

One of the key ways to prioritize your mental health is to make self-care a daily practice. This can include activities such as exercise, meditation, journaling, or simply taking time to relax and unwind. Finding what works best for you and incorporating it into your routine can have a significant impact on your overall mental well-being.

Another important aspect of prioritizing your mental health is seeking professional help when needed. If you are struggling with depression, anxiety, or any other mental health issue, it is important to reach out to a therapist or counselor who can provide you with the support and guidance you need.

Remember, you are not alone in your struggles, and seeking help is a brave and important step towards healing.

In addition to seeking professional help, it is also important to surround yourself with a strong support system of friends and family who can offer you love and encouragement during difficult times. Having a network of people who care about you and understand what you are going through can make a world of difference in your mental health journey.

Lastly, remember to be kind to yourself and practice self-compassion. It is okay to have bad days and to struggle with your mental health from time to time. By treating yourself with the same love and understanding that you would offer to a friend, you can cultivate a sense of resilience and strength that will help you navigate the ups and downs of life with grace and courage. Remember, your mental health matters, and you are worthy of the care and support you need to thrive.

Mental health is a topic that affects us all, but it can be particularly challenging for young people who are navigating the pressures of school, relationships, and the future. It's important for young adults to take control of their mental well-being and prioritize their mental health in order to live a fulfilling and happy life. By inspiring others to take control of their mental well-being, we can create a community of support and understanding for those struggling with mental health issues.

One way to inspire others to take control of their mental well-being is to share your own story. By opening up about your struggles with mental health, you can show others that they are not alone and that it's okay to seek help. Sharing your experiences can also help to break down the stigma surrounding mental health and encourage others to speak up about their own struggles.

Another way to inspire others to take control of their mental well-being is to lead by example. Take care of yourself by prioritizing self-care, getting enough sleep, eating well, and exercising regularly. By showing others that you value your mental health and make it a priority in your life, you can inspire them to do the same.

It's also important to educate others about mental health and the resources available to those struggling with mental health issues. By sharing information about therapy, support groups, hotlines, and other resources, you can empower others to take control of their mental well-being and seek help when they need it.

In conclusion, inspiring others to take control of their mental well-being is crucial for creating a supportive and understanding community for those struggling with mental health issues. By sharing your story, leading by example, and educating others about mental health resources, you can help to break down the stigma surrounding mental health and empower young people to prioritize their mental well-being. Remember, you are not alone in your struggles, and there is help available to support you on your journey to mental wellness.